Wendell MacRae

Wendell MacRae

Photographs: 1927 to 1949

The Witkin Gallery, Inc.
41 East 57th Street
New York, New York 10022

This catalogue was produced in conjunction with the Wendell MacRae exhibition at The Witkin Gallery, Inc., 41 East 57th Street, New York, New York 10022, held September 3 through October 18, 1980.

ISBN 0-937588-00-8 (softbound)
ISBN 0-937588-01-6 (hardbound)

Production coordinated by Linda Lennon
Designed by Karen Skove
Photographs printed for reproduction by Edmund Yankov
Typeset in Linoterm Palatino by Bob McCoy, Cambridge, Mass.
Printed by Eastern Press, Inc., New Haven, Connecticut

This edition consists of 2000 trade copies plus a deluxe, signed, hardbound edition limited to 50, each containing an original, signed, contemporary photograph.

Cover image: *Summer in New York*, ca. 1930
Frontispiece: *Wendell MacRae in the Mojave Desert with his Model T,* self-portrait, 1927

Dear me! Being a great father is either a very difficult or a very sadly unrewarded profession.
Dorothy L. Sayers, *Gaudy Night*

This catalogue is dedicated to a great father and a great photographer

---

to auld acquaintance, ne'er forgot, who aided and abetted his photographic career

Merle Crowell	Cuyler MacRae
Ewing Galloway	Carl Miller
Maxwell M. Geffen	Rudolph Ritter
John Hatlem	DeWitt Wallace
Caroline Hood	Lila Acheson Wallace
Julien Levy	Grace (Gay) Walton
Emma Little	Alice Woodard
Anita Foley MacRae	Claire T. Zyve

and to a new old friend, Lee D. Witkin

Scotia W. MacRae
May 1980

A Remark *by Lee D. Witkin*

Re-discovery of first-rate creativity is one of the true gratifications of being an art dealer. Offering neglected work to the world again on gallery walls provides an excitement that few other professions can equal. When, as in the case of Wendell MacRae, the artist "survives" along with his art, the joy is sweetest. Justice seems to have triumphed and right been restored.

My particular pleasure from Wendell MacRae's photographs comes directly from their being of Manhattan in the 1930s—a time of art deco splendor and harsh depression reality, of Rockefeller Center and Radio City Music Hall rising and the Sixth Avenue elevated coming down— a moment in this mad century of great contrasts and crisis captured by overhead angles and sharp contrasts of light and dark. Here resided all too briefly a singular blend of new elegance and order. The events of the 1940s changed everything. Our Manhattan is no longer that Manhattan. That Manhattan lives on only in cinema, literature, and fine photographs like those of Wendell MacRae.

May 1980

Introduction *by Scotia W. MacRae*

This exhibition had many beginnings, one in 1932 when the Julien Levy Gallery showed photographs of New York by New York photographers, including eight by my father. Forty-five years later, in 1977, seven of them hung on the walls of the Witkin Gallery in an exhibition of prints from the Levy Collection. When I first talked to Lee Witkin about my father's work, he said, "We've been wondering what happened to Wendell MacRae."

During the recession of 1949, the photographic market sagged, so my father decided to take a job at the state college in central Pennsylvania. He once told me he knew too many people in New York who worked so hard to acquire places in the country where they could enjoy their later years that they dropped dead of heart attacks on the verge of retirement. His solution, he says, was to move to the country while he was still able to enjoy it. I am happy to report that he is doing just that.

I have written my father's remembrances from tape-recorded interviews and from my own memories of things he told me. However, I could not supply first-hand information since I appeared late in his New York photographic career. Luckily there is someone who can—my cousin Anita Marie MacRae Feagles. Her parents, Anita and Cuyler (my father's brother), were in business with my father for several years, as was six-year-old Anita Marie. A recently rediscovered document reveals her sentiments at the time:

> My dear tweet-tweet Wendell
> I have made up my mind to be your office girl . . .
> > good luck
> > from your niece
> > braterina MacRae

Her sentiments from historical hindsight can be found on the following pages.

She and I have been on opposite sides of the desk in literary endeavors—she as a creative and prolific writer and I as every author's anathema, an editor. I am more than pleased to be making my debut as a writer in her company.

May 1980

Looking Back: A Foreword *by Anita MacRae Feagles*

When I was a child in the 1930s, for a period of time my home doubled as a photographic studio. The family consisted of my grandmother, Uncle Wendell, my parents, and myself—and every one of us was a model. Asked at school what my father did, I said, "He holds lights for my uncle." Not only was the family used, the house was as well. For months, the doorway from the living room to the dining room was blocked by an enormous man-made spider web. Seeing this, a confused delivery boy said, "Whoever would of thunk it." At one point, there was a daisy chain suspended under the open staircase. At all times, there was a shapely, plastic-like female leg which was not saved only for pictures but kept showing up under and over beds and couches to startle the uninitiated. The basement housed a darkroom, drying prints hung all around the kitchen, and the smell of chemicals was as homey and familiar to me as baking cookies might have been to another child.

Then there were the pictures themselves. It was routine to see huge blowups of my parents in their bathrobes advertising a hotel. And in that picture of the ballerina, I knew my father was invisibly situated under her tutu, where he was holding up her leg. I showed up as the little girl talking to the nice guard at Rockefeller Center, or visiting a school for the blind, or looking rapturous over various foods and toys. It was a particular pleasure to be required to look sullen on one occasion when I was supposed to be a juvenile delinquent being counseled by the kindly social worker. Unfortunately, the county kept that brochure for years, and people looked at me as if I was not the sort of cover girl they really wanted to know.

I spent those years being dressed up and dressed down, posing, listening, watching. There were a great many hours spent under hot lights while Wendell decided whatever he was deciding. Luckily for me, nobody was attempting to teach me anything during all this. But when one is part of a working family, whether it is guided by grocers or acrobats or photographers, one is bound to learn something. What I learned was a permanent distaste for too-conventional households. I also learned that I may as well do what I was supposed to, because although Wendell never verbalized his demand for perfection, it was clear to me even at age six that he wasn't going to settle for anything less. I don't think he knew how to. And that wasn't a bad thing to learn.

May 1980

Seeing the World through My Eyes

by Wendell MacRae as told to Scotia W. MacRae

Portrait of MacRae by David Crerar, 1971

I first realized that a camera could make pictures as beautiful as paintings
when I saw a 1918 photograph by Clarence White reproduced in the *New
York Times Magazine* about 1929 or 1930. It showed the ribs of an ocean-
going wooden ship reaching up toward the clouds in the sky. Entitled
"The Building of Wooden Ships," it struck me then, as now, as beautiful
and full of meaning. Seeing that picture inspired me to want to go out
and do likewise. I was thinking of leaving Ewing Galloway to start on
my own in the photographic business, and Clarence White's image
helped me make up my mind to do so. I still have the clipping I cut out
fifty years ago. Someday I hope to see an original print.

I took my first photographs sometime between the ages of ten and
fourteen. My friend Buz Tormey, a redheaded fellow, had a camera and
let me use it. In a closet turned darkroom in my house, he showed me
how to develop the film. I then persuaded my parents to get me a Box
Brownie camera, and particularly enjoyed taking pictures of the baseball
players at Macalester College, where my father taught. I was especially
proud of a picture I took of a home-run hitter I admired. The Brownie
had a very slow shutter speed — about one-twentieth of a second — so I
had to wait until he had his bat all the way back and push the shutter just
before he slugged the ball. I had a printing frame and got to be pretty

good at making contact prints on Eastman Velox paper.

Later on my cousin, George Payne, who ran a drug store, arranged for me to buy a postcard-sized camera at a good price, but it proved too cumbersome and film was expensive, so I traded it in on a 2¼ x 3¼ Eastman folding camera with a Wollensak lens. My main subjects, aside from my family, were athletic events and the Winter Carnival in St. Paul. The camera had a shutter with an exposure of one-three-hundredth of a second and that was able to stop the motion of the bobsleds traveling downhill at breakneck speeds, the marching bands, each with its distinctive mackinaw, and the ice palace. This was the camera I took with me on my tour of duty in the Marine Corps and later when I went to South America. It was the only camera I had until I left for California in 1927.

My ambition at that point was to become a writer and director of motion pictures. As means to this end I took positions with Paramount Studios, Astoria, Long Island City; and shortly before they closed, with Roland Rogers Productions on Thirty-Third Street, which made films for commercial use.

As a result of my work in the Research Department at Paramount, I spent a lot of time going through the photographs at a place called "The World in Photographs" and became well acquainted with its owner, Ewing Galloway. It was also at Paramount that I learned about lighting by watching the technicians and the cameramen work on the sets in the studios.

At Roland Rogers I was a "cutter" or film editor. He had a good cameraman, Bill Welsh, and a lot of business from companies that wanted films for their showrooms and their traveling salesmen.

When I told Galloway of my intention to go West to work in the motion-picture industry, he proposed that I drive across on the Lincoln Highway, the first coast-to-coast road, and take pictures along the way, which he would buy from me. He wanted photographs that could be used for illustrations for books and magazines. "Saleable" subjects included schools, colleges, monuments, famous buildings, industries, agriculture, street scenes. He sold me a professional camera and tripod at low cost. It was a 5 x 7 folding Cycle-Graphic with a rapid rectilinear lens operated by a bulb. I didn't know how to use it, so he took me over to Bryant Park to photograph a bust of William Cullen Bryant. He showed me how to set up the camera and get the right exposure. Then he took me back to his office to develop the negative. That was the only course, if you can call it that, which I ever had in photography.

While in California, I traded in the Cycle-Graphic on a 5 x 7 Eastman Commercial camera with a 7-inch Goerz Dagor lens. I also acquired a 4 x 5 Graflex camera, which I had until 1948.

I arrived in Hollywood while the studios were trying to make the transition from silent films to talking pictures, and because there were so few films being made, there were no jobs. I supported myself there by taking pictures and sending the film back to Galloway, who paid me $3.00 per negative. Finally he sent me a telegram offering me a position in his firm, so I returned to New York by train.

At Galloway I did a variety of tasks, from mailing out pictures to clients to shooting special assignments, welcome breaks from office routine. One of the people whose work Galloway placed was Burton Holmes, the noted travel lecturer and photographer. One day when Mr. Holmes came into the office, I complimented him on his work. "Thank you," he said, "but the greatest art is selling the picture."

In 1930 I struck out on my own. About then I purchased an Eastman 8 x 10 Commercial camera and a 12-inch Goerz Dagor lens. In 1932 I traded in the 8 x 10 and the 5 x 7, both Eastman cameras, on a Deardorff Commercial 8 x 10 with an auxiliary 5 x 7 back. I continued to use the 12-inch lens and in addition bought a Goerz Hypergon bubble lens, which had an angle of about 130 degrees. Other cameras I used at various times were a 5 x 7 Graflex (1935–1942), a 4 x 5 Deardorff (1940–1949), and a 4 x 5 Speed Graphic (1942–1949). On the 4 x 5 cameras I used the 7-inch and 12-inch Dagor lenses and a Meyer wide-angle lens.

One of my earliest assignments was to photograph a coal mine in Scranton, Pennsylvania, for *World's Work Magazine*. I didn't tell my client that I didn't know how I was going to do the job. I knew nothing about coal mines, except that they could have dangerous gas pockets and sometimes blew up—and the only way to take pictures in the dark was to use magnesium flares, which would probably be forbidden in the mine. Just a few days before I was to leave, General Electric announced that it was placing the first flashbulbs on the market. That saved my gizzard.

The photographs that were exhibited at the Julien Levy Gallery in 1932 attracted favorable critical attention and new clients, including Maxwell M. Geffen, who became my life-long friend. I was told by Mr. Levy's assistant, Allen Porter, that Alfred Stieglitz had come in to see the show. After looking at all the pictures, he came back to mine and commented that they were more imaginative than many of the others. "This one has promise," he concluded.

I didn't know Mr. Stieglitz. I often passed his gallery, called An American Place, and always meant to go in and introduce myself, but I never did. I am very sorry now that I didn't meet him. He gave great impetus to creative photography.

Among the other photographers whose work I admired were Clarence White, Burton Holmes, Lewis Hine, Anton Bruehl, Lusha Nelson, F. S. Lincoln, and Edward Steichen, the leading commercial photographer of the day.

Over the years my clients included magazines, such as the *New York*

Times Magazine, *Fortune*, and *Newsweek*; industries, such as the DuPont Company, the Walter Baker Chocolate Company, the Texas Oil Company; schools and colleges, such as the Fox Meadow School, Riverdale School, Staunton Military Academy, the David Mannes School of Music, Choate School, Manhattanville College, Bard College; businesses such as Maxwell House Coffee and the Julius Kayser Company; social agencies, such as Lavelle School for the Blind, the Guild of the Infant Savior, the Society for the Prevention of Cruelty to Children; and, of course, Rockefeller Center. I also placed murals in the Center, in the *Reader's Digest* offices, in a restaurant, and in the homes of various private clients.

I didn't think of myself as an artist, although I do think that photography is an art. The critics and others who were pushing photography in my day didn't consider you an artist if you made money at it. I enjoyed making pictures whether I took them for my own pleasure or for an assignment. I approached every job with the idea of taking the best possible pictures, no matter what the subject. I wanted to be remembered for doing good work, whatever it was.

A lot of this art lingo is a mystery to me—much of it seems rather precious and out of touch with reality. The statement that best summarizes what I tried to achieve was made by Christopher Morley in his review of my book *Willingly To School*:

> Here . . . appears a book, mostly photographs, so fresh, so sane,
> so truly touching and healthy, so beautiful with the beauty of
> the commonplace, that there is a danger of its being missed.
> This book has heart and soul value; it is the essence of a religion
> that never knew an agnostic; who touches it touches the meaning
> of man.   [*Saturday Review*, 9 February 1935]

Oliver Wendell Holmes, Jr., the Supreme Court Justice, once wrote about the secret, isolated joy of the thinker who knows that hundreds of years hence people will be moving to the measure of his thoughts. I have the secret, isolated joy of hoping that hundreds of years from now, people will be seeing the world through my eyes.

May 1980

List of Plates

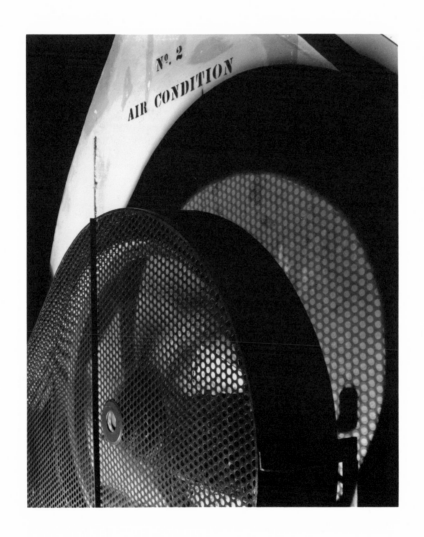

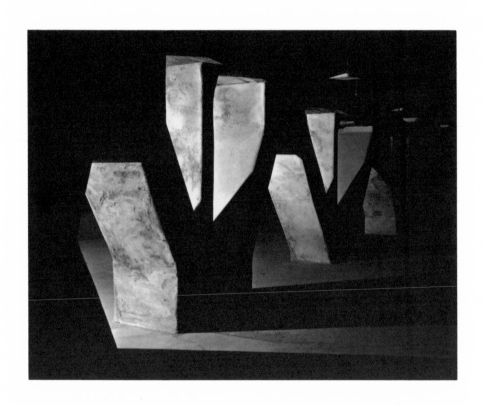

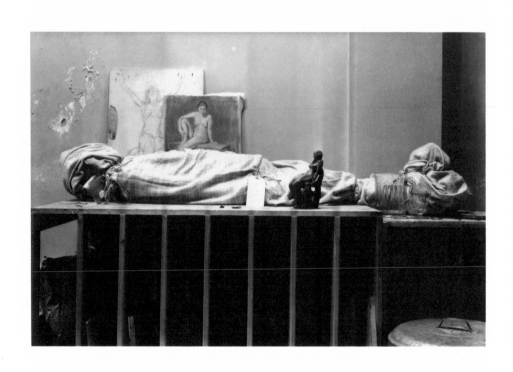

Wendell Scott MacRae: A Chronology

1896	Born 10 July in Metropolis, Illinois, to Mary Scott McRae, a secondary-school teacher, and Farquhar David McRae, a Presbyterian minister and later a professor at Macalester College in St. Paul, Minnesota. Six weeks after the birth of Wendell, their first child, the McRaes moved to Blue Earth, Minnesota. In 1906 they moved to St. Paul.
1910	Graduated from Ramsey Public School, St. Paul.
1910–1912	Attended Macalester Academy.
1912–1914	Attended and graduated from Central High School, St. Paul.
1914–1916	Attended Macalester College. From the fall of 1915 through the summer of 1916, worked as Assistant Sporting Editor at the *St. Paul Pioneer Press*. In the fall of 1916, transferred to the University of Minnesota.
1917	April. Enlisted in the United States Marine Corps as a Private.
1919	June. Resigned commission as First Lieutenant. Re-entered the University of Minnesota in the fall.
1920	Graduated from the University of Minnesota in June. Later that summer, he traveled to New York City with a friend and worked for the DuPont Company organizing stock cards until October, when he sailed to Santo Domingo to work for the United States Military Government, first as Superintendent of Distilleries and later as Purchasing Agent.
1922	June. Left Santo Domingo for New York. In September, sailed for Colombia, South America, to work as wholesaler selling horseshoe nails for the Capewell Horse Nail Company. Traveled on muleback through Colombia, Venezuela, British Guiana, Ecuador, and Trinidad.
1923	Left South America to work at headquarters of Capewell Horse Nail Company, Hartford, Connecticut.
1924	Spring. Began work in Research Department of Paramount Studios, Astoria, Long Island City. Later promoted to Cost-estimating Department.
1926	Summer. Began work for Roland Rogers Productions, a commercial film company, as a "cutter" or film editor.
1927	August. Left for Hollywood to find work in motion-picture business. Arrived November.
1928	May. Left Hollywood for New York. Started work for Ewing Galloway, a photo agency, in June.
1928–1929	Studio and residence at Spuyten Duyvil, 228 Street, Riverdale.
1930	Began own photographic business. Studio and residence at 5040 Tibbett Avenue, Riverdale.
1930–1932	Shared business office with D. J. Culver at 51 East 42 Street. Darkroom work done in Riverdale studio.

1932	June. Exhibition entitled "Photographs of New York by New York Photographers" at Julien Levy Gallery, New York.
1933	Studio in Barbizon Plaza Hotel (roof).
1934–1941	Studio in Rockefeller Center, RKO Building, sixth floor. Changed spelling of name from McRae to MacRae. Studio expropriated by United States Army Intelligence.
1941–1944	Studio and residence at 66 Fifth Avenue in Greenwich Village.
1945	Studio on East 46 Street.
1945–1949	Studio at 25 Vanderbilt Avenue, Grand Central Terminal (top floor).
1949	July. Left New York to become Publications Production Manager at The Pennsylvania State College, State College, Pa. (later The Pennsylvania State University, University Park, Pa.).
1965	Retired from The Pennsylvania State University. Presently residing in State College, Pa.

Additional References

Bath, Gerald Horton, *America's Williamsburg*, photographs by Wendell MacRae (Williamsburg, Virginia: Colonial Williamsburg, 1946).

MacRae, Wendell, *Willingly To School* (New York: Round Table Press, 1934).

Mann, Charles W., Jr., "Wendell MacRae: Expression in Commercial Photography of the 1930s," *History of Photography* 2, no. 2 (April 1978). Reprinted in *Photographer's Forum* 1, no. 2 (February 1979).

Addenda

Vintage Prints of the images in this catalogue as well as other vintage photographs by Wendell MacRae are available through:

The Witkin Gallery, Inc.
41 East 57th Street
New York, New York 10022

All images subject to presale.
Prices upon request.

Contemporary Prints of the images reproduced in this catalogue are also available. They have been printed from the original negatives by Edmund Yankov in 1980, approved and signed by Wendell MacRae, and limited to ten prints per image. They are priced at $300.00 each.

A deluxe, signed, clothbound *Limited Edition* of 50 copies of this catalogue, each containing an original, signed, contemporary photograph is available through the gallery at $150.00.